EXECUTIVE SUMMARY

Angola is a constitutional republic. The ruling Popular Movement for the Liberation of Angola (MPLA) has been in power since independence in 1975. In August 2012, the government held the first presidential and legislative elections following the promulgation of the 2010 constitution. The MPLA received 71.8 percent of the vote, and in September 2012, President Jose Eduardo dos Santos began a five-year term as president under the new constitution.

Civilian authorities generally maintained effective control over the security forces.

The three most important human rights abuses were cruel, excessive, and degrading punishment, including reported cases of torture and beatings; limits on freedoms of assembly, association, speech, and press; and official corruption and impunity.

Other human rights abuses included arbitrary or unlawful deprivation of life; harsh and potentially life-threatening prison conditions; arbitrary arrest and detention; lengthy pretrial detention; impunity for human rights abusers; lack of due process and judicial inefficiency; forced evictions without compensation; restrictions on nongovernmental organizations (NGOs); harassment of and violence against women and children; child labor; trafficking in persons; limits on workers' rights; and forced labor.

The government took some steps to prosecute or punish officials who committed abuses; however, accountability was weak due to a lack of checks and balances, lack of institutional capacity, a culture of impunity, and widespread government corruption.

Section 1. Respect for the Integrity of the Person, Including Freedom from:

a. Arbitrary Deprivation of Life and other Unlawful or Politically Motivated Killings

In carrying out law enforcement activities, the government or its agents used excessive and sometimes deadly force.

For example, on August 6, security force members reportedly shot and killed a 14-year-old boy, Rufino Antonio, after they demolished his family's and other allegedly illegally built homes in a suburban Luanda zone, according to media sources and several NGOs (see section 1.e.). The government and the national ombudsman launched separate investigations into the shooting death, both of which remained ongoing at year's end.

On April 5, the Huambo provincial court sentenced Jose Kalupeteka, the leader of the Light of the World religious sect, to 28 years in prison for the 2015 clashes between members of his group and police that left 13 civilians and nine police officers dead, according to official figures, although opposition parties continued to allege a higher casualty rate. On August 9, new clashes between police and Light of the World followers in Kwanza Sul Province reportedly resulted in the deaths of five church members and three police officers, and a similar confrontation on August 13 resulted in an unknown number of casualties. The government stated the Attorney General's Office (PGR) was investigating.

On August 21, media reported that an officer of Alfa 5 Security Services, a private security company affiliated with the government's diamond enterprise, Endiama, allegedly killed 17-year-old Gabriel Mufugueno, in Lucapa, Lunda Norte Province. According to a relative of the victim, police detained the Alfa 5 officer allegedly responsible for the shooting. The incident elicited protests from artisanal miners in the area.

b. Disappearance

There were no reports of politically motivated disappearances.

c. Torture and Other Cruel, Inhuman, or Degrading Treatment or Punishment

The constitution and law prohibit all forms of torture and cruel, inhuman, or degrading treatment or punishment, but the government did not always enforce these prohibitions. Periodic reports of beatings and other abuses of persons on the way to and in police stations during interrogations continued. The government acknowledged that at times members of the security forces used excessive force when apprehending individuals. Police authorities openly condemned some acts of violence or excessive force against individuals and asked that victims report abuses to the national police or the Office of the Public Defender (Ombudsman).

On September 1, Jose Padrao Loureiro, suspected of belonging to a gang, was beaten and killed by police inside Rangel Police Station, following his arrest on August 31, according to press reports. During the one-day detention, Loureiro was allegedly tortured and killed. National Police Spokesperson Mateus Rodrigues said an autopsy revealed the victim was severely beaten. Authorities opened an investigation on September 5 and detained five police officers.

Security forces reacted harshly and sometimes violently to public demonstrations against the government. Several media and NGO accounts reported police around the country, in particular in the provinces of Luanda, Malanje, Benguela, and the city of Lobito, beat protesters. The visible presence of security forces was enough to deter significantly what were deemed by the government to be unlawful demonstrations. Authorities claimed known agitators who sought only to create social instability organized many of the public demonstrations.

The media reported that, on August 20, during a protest in Luanda calling for the resignation of President dos Santos and for the release of activist Dago Nivel, police allegedly beat several protesters and used the police canine brigade to disrupt the protest; dogs wounded three protesters. The media provided photographs of the incident, including of men with visible bite wounds. Police reportedly later drove a group of protesters, including the men wounded by the canine brigade, to the outskirts of the city and left them there. The General Command of the National Police denied any knowledge of the case.

There were reports of abuses by private security companies in diamond producing regions.

For example, on April 21, in the Cafunfo diamond area, in Lunda-Norte province, private security guards working for a private company allegedly severely beat 10 artisanal miners with machetes, according to a media report that included a video of the incident.

Prison and Detention Center Conditions

Prison and detention center conditions were harsh and potentially life threatening. Domestic NGOs, activists, and the media continued to highlight corruption, violence, overcrowding, a lack of medical care, and generally poor conditions.

Physical Conditions: In April Antonio Fortunato, director general of penitentiary services, acknowledged overcrowding in prisons was a serious problem.

Authorities frequently held pretrial detainees with sentenced inmates, and short-term detainees with those serving long-term sentences for violent crimes, especially in provincial prisons.

Prison conditions varied widely between urban and rural areas. Prisons in rural areas were less crowded and reportedly had better rehabilitation, training, and reintegration services. Prisons did not always provide adequate medical care, sanitation, potable water, or food, and it was customary for families to bring food to prisoners. Local NGOs stated prison services were insufficient. In 2015 Fortunato acknowledged that approximately five prisoners died each month in the country's prisons from diseases such as HIV/AIDS, malaria, and tuberculosis.

In April, Fortunato acknowledged that Viana Jail (on the outskirts of Luanda) lacked adequate potable water and food for inmates. On September 14, activist Nuno Dala published photos allegedly taken inside Viana Jail depicting severely overcrowded conditions and several inmates suffering from malnutrition and tuberculosis due to a lack of food and potable water. On September 16, the newspaper *Novo Jornal* published a report on the allegedly deplorable conditions; the report included photographs of prisoners who appeared to be malnourished. *Novo Jornal* also reported that the Rapid Intervention Police (PIR) and the Special Prison Services Detachment (DESP) tortured one of the prisoners allegedly for his role in sharing photos with persons outside the jail. Observers generally regard the newspaper as credible; however, its reporting on conditions inside Viana Jail could not be independently verified.

According to a press report, female inmates accused two officials from the Human Resources and Penal Control Units of the Kwanza Sul Jail of coercing them to have sex in order to be released from prison under the new Amnesty Law. Authorities launched an investigation, and on September 26, the PGR announced the investigation concluded the claims of sexual abuse were false and there were no irregularities in the prison's inmate release procedures.

<u>Administration</u>: The Ministry of Interior claimed that adequate statistics were available in each facility and that authorities were able to locate every prisoner.

The government investigated and monitored prison and detention center conditions. There was no prison ombudsperson.

Some offenders, including violent offenders, reported paying fines and bribes to secure their freedom but it was unclear how prevalent this practice was.

<u>Independent Monitoring</u>: The government permitted visits to prisons by independent local and international human rights observers and foreign diplomats. For example, the government permitted foreign diplomats to visit the "15 + 2" activists during their imprisonment (section 1.d.). Nevertheless, civil society organizations faced difficulties in contacting detainees, and prison authorities undermined civil society work in the prisons.

Members of opposition parties visited prisons around the country on a regular basis and reported uneven improvements in living conditions and rehabilitation programs. A local NGO that provides pro bono legal services to inmates said prison officials were trying to improve conditions but overcrowding limited results. According to the Ministry of Justice and Human Rights, the ministry made monthly visits to detention centers with representatives of the Office of the Public Defender, the PGR, and members of the National Assembly to assess prisoners' living conditions.

d. Arbitrary Arrest or Detention

The law prohibits arbitrary arrest and detention; however, security forces did not always respect these prohibitions.

According to several NGO and civil society sources, police arbitrarily arrested individuals without due process and routinely detained persons who participated, or were about to participate, in antigovernment protests, despite this right being protected by the constitution. They often released the detainees after a few hours. For example, on August 21, in Lobito, police beat and arrested activists Paulo Vinte-Cinco and Francisco Catraio of the Revolutionary Movement while they participated in a weekly meeting with other youth to discuss politics. More than 20 police officers broke up the meeting and dispersed the participants. Police released the two activists the next day.

Role of the Police and Security Apparatus

The national police, controlled by the Ministry of Interior, are responsible for internal security and law enforcement. The Expatriate and Migration Services (SME), also in the Ministry of Interior, is responsible for migration law enforcement. The state intelligence and security service reports to the presidency and investigates sensitive state security matters. The Angolan Armed Forces (FAA) are responsible for external security but also had domestic security responsibilities, including border security, expulsion of irregular migrants, and small-scale actions against Front for the Liberation of the Enclave of Cabinda separatists in Cabinda.

Civilian authorities maintained effective control over the FAA and the national police, and the government has mechanisms to investigate and punish abuse and corruption. The security forces generally were effective, although sometimes brutal, at maintaining stability. The national police and FAA have internal mechanisms to investigate security force abuses, and the government provided some training to reform the security forces. Impunity for security force abuses remained a problem, however.

Local population generally welcomed police presence in neighborhoods and on streets as enhancing general safety and security. Police officers, however, were believed routinely to extort civilians to supplement their income. Corruption and impunity remained serious problems. The national police handled most complaints internally through opaque disciplinary procedures, which sometimes led to formal punishment including dismissal. The national police participated in a television series designed to show a gamut of interactions between police and civilians. The goal of the show was to encourage the population to collaborate with police while discouraging security force members' procurement of bribes or their payment. The PGR has an anticorruption unit, charged with oversight of police wrongdoing. The government disclosed publicly the results of some investigations that led to disciplinary action. On September 17, authorities terminated two police officers for extorting money from drivers during traffic stops, according to a press report. On September 13, the government announced the deployment of 400 newly trained police officers as part of an effort to eliminate corruption from the police force.

Police participated in professional training with law enforcement officials from several countries in the region.

Arrest Procedures and Treatment of Detainees

In December 2015 a new law on pretrial procedures (Law 25/15) entered into force.

The law requires a magistrate or judge to issue a warrant before an arrest may be made, although a person caught committing an offense may be arrested immediately without a warrant. Authorities, however, did not always procure warrants before making an arrest.

By law the public prosecutor must inform the detainee of the legal basis for his or her detention within 48 hours; however, NGO sources reported authorities often did not respect this requirement. If the public prosecutor is unable to determine whether there is a legal basis for the detention within 48 hours, the prosecutor has the authority to release the person or, depending on the seriousness of the case, require the person to submit to one or more pretrial procedures prescribed by law such as posting bail, periodic appearance before authorities, or house arrest.

If the public prosecutor determines a legal basis exists for the detention, a person can be held in pretrial detention for up to four months without charge and up to 12 months before a judge is required to rule on the case. Cases of special complexity regarding crimes punishable by eight or more years allow for pretrial detention without charge for up to six months and up to 14 months before a judge is required to rule on the case. Under the law, the period of pretrial detention counts toward the total amount of time served.

The law states that all detainees have the right to a lawyer, either chosen by them or appointed by the government on a pro-bono basis. The lack of lawyers in certain provinces at times impeded this right. On September 24, the head of the Angolan Bar Association (ABA) stated there were 1,700 lawyers in the country, an insufficient number to handle the volume of criminal cases, and the geographical distribution of lawyers throughout the country was a problem, as most lawyers were concentrated in Luanda. In 2015 the Ministry of Justice and Human Rights reported that all municipal courts were staffed with licensed lawyers, but at the same time recognized access to a lawyer, especially in the provinces and in rural areas, remained a problem. Several lawyers and NGOs noted that even in Luanda most poor defendants do not have access to lawyers during their first appearance before a judicial authority or during their trial.

The law allows family members prompt access to detainees, but prison officials occasionally ignored this right or made it conditional upon payment of a bribe. The law requires detainees be held incommunicado for up to 48 hours until being presented to a public prosecutor, except they may communicate with their lawyer or a family member.

A functioning but ineffective bail system, widely used for minor crimes, existed. Prisoners and their families reported that prison officials demanded bribes to release prisoners.

Arbitrary Arrest: Unlawful arrest and detention remained serious problems. According to the PGR, allegations of government wrongdoing on arrest practices made by local and international NGOs were due to a lack of understanding of national laws.

Pretrial Detention: Excessively long pretrial detention continued to be a serious problem. An inadequate number of judges and poor communication among authorities contributed to the problem. In some cases, authorities held inmates in prison for up to two years before their trials began. The Ministry of Interior reported during the year that 11,000 inmates were pretrial detainees, approximately 45 percent of the total inmate population. The government often did not release detainees confined beyond the legal time limit, claiming previous releases of pretrial detainees had resulted in an increase in crime.

Detainees' Ability to Challenge Lawfulness of Detention before a Court: The constitution provides the right of habeas corpus to citizens to challenge their detention before a court. On June 29, the Supreme Court granted the group of activists known as the "15+2" a writ of habeas corpus, ruling that following their March conviction and sentencing to between two and eight years in prison by the Luanda Provincial Court the appeal lodged by their lawyers had a suspensive effect and required their release pending the outcome of their appeal. Judge Domingos Januario, the judge of first instance for the Luanda Provincial Court, was later accused of concealing the activists' petition for habeas corpus from the Supreme Court. The attorney general launched an investigation of the judge's handling of the case, which remained ongoing as of September.

The case against the "15+2" began in June 2015 in Luanda, when 15 activists were arrested by security forces during a book discussion. In September 2015, after 102 days of pretrial detention, they and two other individuals were charged with engaging in "preparatory acts to incite rebellion and for planning the overthrow of the president and other institutions of the state." The activists are collectively referred to as the "15+2." The Ministry of Justice and Human Rights and the PGR claimed the legal process to detain and charge the activists had been conducted within the law.

<u>Amnesty</u>: On July 20, the National Assembly passed the Amnesty Law (11/16), providing a general amnesty to criminals convicted prior to November 11, 2015, of nonviolent crimes whose sentences were 12 or fewer years in prison. Government representatives stated that the law, proposed by the president in honor of the country's fortieth anniversary of independence in 2015, was also intended to ease overcrowding in prisons. As of September 23, more than 2,500 prisoners were released under the new law.

e. Denial of Fair Public Trial

The constitution and law provide for an independent and impartial judiciary. Institutional weaknesses in the judicial system, however, such as political influence in the decision-making process, were problems. The Ministry of Justice and Human Rights and the PGR worked to improve the independence of prosecutors and judges. The National Institute for Judicial Studies conducted capacity-building programs on the importance of an independent judicial system.

There were long trial delays at the Supreme Court. Criminal courts also had a large backlog of cases, which resulted in major delays in hearings. There were only 22 municipal courts for 163 municipalities. To increase access to justice, the PGR in 2014 established offices of legal counsel in most municipalities.

Informal courts remained the principal institutions through which citizens resolved civil conflicts in rural areas, such as disputes over a bartering deal. Each community in which informal courts were located established local rules, creating disparities in how similar cases were resolved from one community to the next. Traditional leaders (known as "sobas") also heard and decided local civil cases. Sobas do not have the authority to resolve criminal cases; only courts can hear criminal cases.

Both the national police and the FAA have internal court systems that generally remained closed to outside scrutiny. Although members of these organizations can be tried under their internal regulations, cases that include violations of criminal or civil laws can also fall under the jurisdiction of provincial courts. Both the PGR and the Ministry of Justice and Human Rights have civilian oversight responsibilities over military courts.

In November 2015 the judge presiding over the case of the "15+2" activists charged with "preparatory acts to incite rebellion and for planning the overthrow of the president and other institutions of the state" ordered closure of the public trial to independent observers such as members of the diplomatic corps and local NGOs due to the high level of interest in the proceedings and space constraints. Attendance by the public was limited to two family members per defendant. He made special accommodations for reporters to follow the trial in a separate room via closed circuit television. Independent observers were present in other high-profile and sensitive trials such as the 2015 libel and defamation case of Rafael Marques and the 2015 rebellion case against Marcos Mavungo.

Trial Procedures

Although the law provides all citizens the right to a fair trial, authorities did not always respect this right. Defendants enjoy the right to a presumption of innocence until proven guilty. Authorities must inform defendants of the charges levied against them in detail within 48 hours of their detention. Defendants have the right to free language interpretation during all legal proceedings from the moment charged through all appeals. By law trials are usually public, although each court has the right to close proceedings. Defendants have the right to be present and consult with an attorney, either chosen by them or appointed by the state, in a timely manner. According to the Ministry of Justice and Human Rights, all public defenders are licensed lawyers. Defendants do not have the right to confront their accusers. They may question witnesses against them and present witnesses and evidence on their own behalf. Defendants have the right to sufficient time and facilities to prepare a defense. The law protects defendants from providing self-incriminating testimony. Individuals have the right to appeal their convictions. Authorities did not always respect these trial procedure rights.

Defendants and their attorneys have the right to access government-held evidence relevant to their cases, but authorities did not always uphold this right. For example, in March 2015 political activist Marcos Mavungo was arrested on suspicion of plotting an act of violence against the provincial government of Cabinda. In September 2015, more than 200 days after his arrest, Mavungo was convicted of charges of rebellion against the state and sentenced to six years in prison. His lawyers complained publicly they did not have access to the evidence the government claimed it had to prove guilt; however, the Ministry of Justice and Human Rights and the PGR stated that Mavungo's case was conducted within appropriate parameters for a case involving national security and that the sentence reflected the seriousness of the crime. Mavungo appealed his sentence. On May 20, the Supreme Court ruled in his favor, acquitting the activist of the charge of rebellion against the state. The Supreme Court cited in its ruling a lack of sufficient evidence to uphold the charge.

A separate juvenile court is designated for children's affairs. The juvenile court hears cases of minors between the ages of 12 and 16 accused of committing a criminal offense. Minors over age 16 accused of committing a criminal offense are tried in regular courts. In many rural municipalities, there is no provision for juvenile courts, so offenders as young as 12 can be tried as adults. In many cases traditional leaders have state authority to resolve disputes and determine punishments for civil offenses, including offenses committed by juveniles. Traditional authorities are defined in the constitution as ad hoc units of the state.

The president appoints Supreme Court justices for life terms without confirmation by the National Assembly. The Supreme Court generally hears cases concerning alleged political and security crimes.

Political Prisoners and Detainees

The Ministry of Justice and Human Rights denied there were political prisoners in the country. Opposition political parties, however, often claimed their members were detained because of their political affiliations. Media reports of opposition parties' members being harassed and detained for up to 48 hours were common but difficult to confirm.

Civil Judicial Procedures and Remedies

Damages for human rights violations may be sought in municipal or provincial courts and appealed to the Supreme Court.

Property Restitution

The constitution recognizes the right to housing and quality of life, and the law states that persons relocated should receive fair compensation. Under the constitution all untitled land belongs to the state. Throughout the year the government used eminent domain laws to raze housing settlements and other buildings to carry out urban redevelopment projects. According to NGO sources and multiple press reports, security forces demolished hundreds of allegedly illegal, privately built homes in Zango, a suburban Luanda zone that falls within the restrictive perimeter of the Luanda-Bengo Economic zone. These demolitions reportedly displaced thousands of persons and resulted in several deaths during the year. In addition to the shooting death of a 14-year-old boy in August (section 1.a.), the demolitions resulted in the accidental decapitation of an infant in April and the deaths of two individuals with medical conditions in August. Some persons forced to move did not receive fair compensation, at times due to lack of clear title or permits for the destroyed property. Relocated persons who received new housing units often complained their units were located far from their jobs or places of business, or were of substandard quality. There was no new information on the status of a 2015 investigation into reports security forces harassed activists working for SOS Habitat, an NGO dealing with land rights.

f. Arbitrary or Unlawful Interference with Privacy, Family, Home, or Correspondence

The constitution and law prohibit such actions, but the government did not always respect these prohibitions. Civil organizations and politically active individuals, including government critics, members of opposition parties, and journalists, complained the government maintained surveillance of their activities and membership. These groups also frequently complained of threats and harassment based on their affiliations with groups that were purportedly or explicitly antigovernment. On July 29, Monica Almeida, the wife of "15+2" activist Luaty Beirao, was stopped by two police vehicles while driving in Luanda. Almeida alleged that police blocked her cell phone to prevent her from calling for help and ordered her to drive with the police vehicles for three hours as they proceeded aimlessly around the city, according to press reports. The police responsible later claimed they had mistaken Almeida for a suspected criminal and announced an investigation into the incident.

Section 2. Respect for Civil Liberties, Including:

a. Freedom of Speech and Press

The constitution and law provide for freedom of speech and press; however, state dominance of most media outlets and self-censorship by journalists limited the practical application of these rights. Most private media organizations were located in the capital.

<u>Freedom of Speech and Expression</u>: Individuals reported practicing self-censorship but generally were able to criticize government policies without fear of direct reprisal. Social media was widely used in the larger cities and provided an open forum for discussion. There are no laws restricting the use or content of social media.

<u>Press and Media Freedoms</u>: Private radio and print media criticized the government openly and harshly. Authorities occasionally threatened journalists and publishers with harassment and arrest for covering sensitive stories. Journalists routinely complained of lack of transparency and communication from government press offices and other government officials. This often led to one-sided reporting, with opposition and civil society figures frequently voicing their opinions in privately owned media outlets while government officials kept silent even on noncontroversial issues. During the year, the government created a senior-level department to coordinate government communication with the media and established the practice of weekly briefings during which journalists could question a government minister. The briefings were broadcast on television and radio.

Official news outlets, including Angolan Public Television, Radio Nacional, and the *Jornal de Angola* newspaper, favored the ruling party and gave only limited coverage to opposition political parties. Opposition parties received only limited coverage of their legislative participation in the National Assembly. During the year, however, official news outlets made a noticeable effort to include opposition party members and other commentators in nationally televised debates on issues such as politics, the rule of law, and the economy.

<u>Violence and Harassment</u>: Authorities arrested, harassed, and intimidated journalists. For example, on August 30, security forces stopped a team of journalists from the newspaper *Novo Jornal* driving within the Zango demolition site (section 1.e.), according to an article published in the newspaper September 2. Security force members allegedly searched the journalists' vehicle and confiscated their belongings. They then allegedly transported the journalists in a military vehicle and threatened to beat and try them in court. One journalist allegedly was beaten. The security force members released the journalists after six hours and returned their belongings, with the exception of a video camera and 20,000 kwanza ($118).

<u>Censorship or Content Restrictions</u>: Journalists practiced self-censorship. Security force members at times did not allow journalists to digitally record police violence against civilians. For example, on May 24, journalist and foreign news service stringer Coque Mukuta was beaten and detained by local police outside of Luanda, after witnessing an altercation between street vendors (zungeiras), police, and Criminal Investigation Service agents and trying to interview one of the street vendors involved in the incident. Mukuta alleged that police forced him into a

police vehicle, beat him, confiscated his possessions, and detained him for 12 hours. Mukuta filed a formal complaint against the policeman who beat him.

The minister of social communication, spokesperson of the presidency, and the national director of information maintained significant decision-making authority over the media. It was commonly understood these individuals actively vetted news stories in the state-controlled print, television, and radio media and exercised considerable authority over some privately owned outlets. State-controlled media and private media outlets owned by those close to the government rarely published or broadcast stories critical of the ruling party, government officials, or government policies.

Libel/Slander Laws: Defamation is a crime punishable by imprisonment or a fine, and unlike in most cases in which defendants are presumed innocent until proven guilty (see section 1.e.), defendants in defamation cases have the burden of proving their innocence by providing evidence of the validity of the allegedly damaging material.

Several journalists in print media, radio, and political blogs faced libel and defamation lawsuits. Journalists complained the government used libel laws to limit their ability to report on corruption and nepotistic practices. According to the PGR, some journalists abused their positions and published inaccurate stories about government officials without verifying the facts or providing the accused the right of reply. In May 2015, a judge found journalist and human rights activist Rafael Marques guilty of criminal libel and gave him a six-month suspended sentence, which could be reinstated at any point up to two years from the date of sentencing if Marques committed another crime.

Internet Freedom

The government did not restrict or disrupt access to the internet or censor online content, and there were no credible reports the government monitored private online communications without appropriate legal oversight. According to the International Telecommunication Union, in 2015 approximately 12 percent of residents had access to the internet. In 2014 the government started the program Angola On-line, a free Wi-Fi service.

Academic Freedom and Cultural Events

There were no government restrictions on academic freedom or cultural events.

b. Freedom of Peaceful Assembly and Association

Freedom of Assembly

The constitution and law provide for the right of assembly, but the government regularly restricted this right.

The law requires written notification to the local administrator and police three days before public assemblies are to be held. For public assemblies during a workday, the law requires the events to start after 7 p.m. The law, however, does not require government permission for such events. The government at times prohibited events based on perceived or claimed security considerations. Police and administrators did not interfere with progovernment gatherings. Nonpartisan groups intending to criticize the government or government leaders, however, often met a heavy police presence and government excuses preventing them from holding the event. Usually authorities claimed the timing or venue requested was problematic or that the proper authorities had not received notification.

According to press reports and NGO sources, on July 23, police detained 35 members of the protest movement "Revolutionary Movement" or "Revus" in Benguela as they traveled to a demonstration to protest the rising price of food in the province. The governor of Benguela denied the request to organize the protest, but the organizers decided to proceed, and police set up checkpoints on main roads to intercept and detain protesters. Police released the protesters the same day.

The government at times arbitrarily restricted the activities of associations it considered subversive by refusing to grant permits for organized activities. Opposition parties generally were permitted to organize and hold meetings; nevertheless, opposition officials continued to report obstructions to the free exercise of their parties' right to meet.

Freedom of Association

The constitution and law provide for the right of association, but the government did not always respect this right (see also section 7.a.). Extensive delays in the NGO registration process continued to be a problem. NGOs that had not yet received registration were nevertheless allowed to operate.

The government published a new NGO regulation in March 2015 that civil society criticized as potentially restrictive and intrusive. For example, the new regulation requires NGOs to obtain approval from the government before the implementation of any project, imposes local authorities as the supervisors of NGO projects within their municipalities, and requires frequent financial reports of NGO activities to the government. The government stated this regulation is part of its strategy to combat money-laundering and terrorist financing.

c. Freedom of Religion

See the Department of State's *International Religious Freedom Report* at www.state.gov/religiousfreedomreport/.

d. Freedom of Movement, Internally Displaced Persons, Protection of Refugees, and Stateless Persons

The constitution and law provide for freedom of internal movement, foreign travel, emigration, and repatriation; however, the government at times restricted these rights.

Abuse of Migrants, Refugees, and Stateless Persons: The government sometimes cooperated with the Office of the UN High Commissioner for Refugees (UNHCR), the International Organization for Migration, and other humanitarian organizations in providing protection and assistance to internally displaced persons (IDPs), refugees, returning refugees, asylum seekers, stateless persons, or other persons of concern. UN Special Rapporteur on the human rights of migrants, Francois Crepeau, visited the country at the invitation of the government from May 3-10. Crepeau's report, issued subsequent to his visit, criticized the government for its lack of adequate protections for refugees, asylum seekers, and migrants and cited government failure to implement key elements of the 2015 Asylum Law, which had the effect of impeding refugee and asylum seekers' access to basic services and documents such as birth certificates for children of foreign-born parents. Several NGOs that work with refugee populations also cited security force harassment of the refugee and asylum seeker community. In diamond-rich Lunda Norte Province, NGOs and the media reported several acts of violence and degrading treatment, including rape and sexual abuse of Congolese migrants. In response to the allegations of sexual violence, President dos Santos created a commission that included UN representatives to improve the situation around the borders. The commission performed regular verification missions to assess progress at the border crossing points.

<u>In-country Movement</u>: Police maintained roadside checkpoints throughout the country. Reports by local NGOs suggested some police officers extorted money from civilians at checkpoints and during regular traffic stops. Reports from the diamond mining provinces of Lunda Norte and Lunda Sul indicated some government agents restricted the movements of local communities.

In 2013 the Angolan and the Democratic Republic of the Congo (DRC) governments agreed on a special laissez-passer program for their nationals that allows for increased legal movement of persons and products between Lunda Norte and the DRC province then known as Katanga.

<u>Emigration and Repatriation</u>: In 2012 UNHCR and regional governments agreed to a cessation of prima facie refugee status for Angolans on the grounds that asylum and protection for most Angolans was no longer required. On September 30, the Ministry of Assistance and Social Integration stated the government would no longer acknowledge refugee status for citizens living outside of the country, citing the completion of its voluntary repatriation program, which allowed 525,871 citizens to return between 2003 and 2015. During the year Angolan former refugees returned spontaneously from Zambia and the DRC.

Protection of Refugees

The government did not provide adequate protection to refugees and asylum seekers.

<u>Access to Asylum</u>: The Asylum Law provides specific procedures for the submission of an asylum application and guidance on the determination of asylum and refugee cases. UNHCR and several NGOs reported that the law did not function in practice during the year and asylum seekers and refugees did not have a mechanism to apply for or resolve their status. The law changed the role of the Committee for the Recognition of the Right to Asylum (COREDA), the former implementing mechanism to identify, verify, and legalize asylum seekers, to that of an advisory board; however, by September the government had not put into practice an alternative mechanism to adjudicate asylum and refugee cases in COREDA's place. The law also established the creation of reception centers for refugees and asylum seekers where they are supposed to receive assistance until the government makes a decision on their cases. There were three reception centers.

<u>Employment</u>: Formal restrictions on a refugee's ability to seek employment existed. Regulation 273/13 restricted refugees from obtaining the mandatory business license, "Alvara commercial," required to own and operate a business. Refugees often faced difficulty obtaining employment due inability to obtain legal documents required to work in the formal sector. These difficulties were compounded by a general lack of acceptance of the refugee card and lack of knowledge about the rights it was intended to safeguard.

<u>Access to Basic Services</u>: Persons with recognized refugee status could at times obtain public services; however, UNHCR, NGOs, and refugees reported that refugees were unable to obtain legal documents following passage of the Asylum Law and at times faced difficulty accessing public services such as health care and education. Corruption by officials compounded these difficulties.

Section 3. Freedom to Participate in the Political Process

The constitution and law provide citizens the ability to choose their government through free and fair periodic elections based on universal and equal suffrage and conducted by secret ballot guaranteeing the free expression of the will of the people. Citizens exercised this ability at the national level, but did not have that ability at the provincial or municipal levels.

According to the 2010 constitution, presidential and legislative elections should be held every five years. In 2012 citizens elected legislative representatives and the president. The constitution calls for the first-ever local elections; however, the right to elect local leaders remained restricted, and local elections did not occur.

Elections and Political Participation

<u>Recent Elections</u>: In 2012 the government held legislative elections and the country's first postwar presidential election. The ruling MPLA won 71.8 percent of the vote in the legislative elections. Domestic and international observers reported polling throughout the country was peaceful and generally credible, although the ruling party enjoyed advantages due to state control of major media and other resources. Opposition parties contested aspects of the electoral process and the results but accepted their seats in the National Assembly. In 2012 the constitutional court rejected opposition appeals and certified the election results as free and fair.

The central government appoints the provincial governors, and the constitution does not specify a timeline for implementing municipal-level elections. By year's end, government and ruling party officials had not announced a target date for the municipal elections postponed in 2015. Opposition parties and some members of civil society were dissatisfied with the slow pace and claimed the ruling party lacked the political will to organize municipal elections.

<u>Political Parties and Political Participation</u>: The ruling MPLA party dominated all political institutions. Political power was concentrated in the presidency and the Council of Ministers, through which the president exercised executive power. The council can enact laws, decrees, and resolutions, assuming most functions normally associated with the legislative branch. The National Assembly consists of 220 deputies elected under a party list proportional representation system. This body has the authority to draft, debate, and pass legislation, but the executive branch often proposed and drafted legislation for the assembly's approval. After the 2012 legislative elections, opposition deputies held 20 percent of parliamentary seats, up from 13 percent in 2008.

Political parties must be represented in all 18 provinces, but only the MPLA, UNITA, and the Broad Convergence for the Salvation of Angola, to a lesser extent, had truly national constituencies. By law no political party could limit party membership based on ethnicity, race, or gender.

Several altercations between MPLA and opposition parties' supporters reportedly occurred during the year. On May 25, a delegation comprising UNITA parliamentarians and local party representatives was attacked in Benguela Province, allegedly by MPLA supporters and local residents, resulting in the deaths of four individuals, including two MPLA supporters and one UNITA supporter. UNITA initiated a parliamentary inquiry into the incident. The Ministry of the Interior referred the case to the PGR, which launched an investigation. On July 1-2, a UNITA party office in the Ramiros neighborhood of Luanda was vandalized and the party flag burned. UNITA party officials and several press reports alleged the vandals responsible were MPLA supporters. On July 1, President dos Santos publicly called on political parties, citizens, and associations to avoid engaging in political intolerance and report incidents of intolerance to appropriate authorities. Opposition politicians alleged a lack of interest by the national police, especially in the provinces, to investigate alleged violence against opposition political parties. The Ministry of Justice and Human Rights stated many of the complaints by opposition parties were under investigation.

<u>Participation of Women and Minorities</u>: There are no laws limiting the participation of women and minorities in the political process and women and minorities did participate. Of the 220 deputies in the national assembly, 79 were women. Two women served as governors (out of 18 nationwide), and five women were cabinet ministers (out of 35). The country has multiple linguistic groups, many of which were represented in government.

Section 4. Corruption and Lack of Transparency in Government

Although the law provides criminal penalties for official corruption, the government did not implement these laws effectively, and local and international NGOs and media sources reported officials engaged in corrupt practices with impunity.

<u>Corruption</u>: Government corruption at all levels was widespread, and accountability was limited due to a lack of checks and balances, lack of institutional capacity, and a culture of impunity, although there were some institutions working to improve transparency and accountability within the government. The judiciary was subject to political influence and conflict of interest. Public prosecutions of corruption cases were rare.

On March 1, the Office of the Inspector General (OIG) for the Global Fund, an international organization focused on fighting HIV/AIDS, tuberculosis, and malaria, published the findings from a corruption investigation related to a 2013 malaria grant to the government. The OIG reported that senior Ministry of Health officials committed fraud and collusion by diverting several million dollars of Global Fund grant money into their own private investments. The Ministry of Health required that the officials repay the funds, which the Global Fund reported were later repaid, and referred the case for prosecution. There was no public information on the status of the case at year's end.

The Ministry of Finance published the national budget including information on national expenditures and debt obligations, on its website. Accountability of public funds expenditure, however, remained poor. During the year the Ministry of Finance and the International Monetary Fund collaborated on financial transparency initiatives.

In June 2015 the National Assembly passed the Mutual Legal Assistance Law, which allows government agencies and private companies to share information with international law enforcement agencies to combat money laundering and the financing of terrorism. In 2012 the government decided to pursue structural anti-money-laundering (AML) reforms. In support of this strategy, the country joined the International Co-operation Review Group (ICRG) established by the Financial Action Task Force (FATF), an intergovernmental "policy-making" body responsible for setting standards and implementing necessary measures to combat money laundering, terrorist financing and other threats to the integrity of the international financial system. The government worked with ICRG as well as the regional FATF group to which it belongs, the Eastern and Southern Africa Anti-Money Laundering Group (ESAAMLG), to conform its laws, regulations, and organizations to FATF's recommendations, and adopted a mutual evaluation report (MER) on antimoney laundering and countering the financing of terrorism (AML/CFT) deficiencies to be addressed. For its efforts in addressing these deficiencies, the country was removed from the FATF/ICRG gray list in February, with the goal to continue working with the ESAAMLG to address the full range of AML/CFT deficiencies. In August, however, the ESAAMLG Task Force of Senior Officials reported the country had not made significant progress and had failed to implement the MER recommendations since August 2015.

While the National Bank of Angola (BNA) announced a series of actions to implement stronger AML/CFT measures, many local and international financial sector commentators noted that the BNA lacked sufficient oversight on AML/CFT issues. Experts point to the persistent lack of coordination across the country's financial and law enforcement agencies on identifying and ultimately prosecuting financial sector crimes. Despite the ESAAMLG's recommendation to the government to increase the role, independence, and visibility of the country's five-year-old Financial Intelligence Unit (FIU), the FIU largely continued to operate in the shadow of the BNA and relied on the BNA for its budget. The Anti-Corruption Group, formed in 2013 and chaired by the Ministry of Justice, met infrequently and did not make public its findings during the year.

As in previous years there were credible reports government officials used their political positions to profit from business deals. The business environment continued to favor those connected to the government, including members of the president's family.

Government ministers and other high-level officials commonly and openly owned interests in public and private companies regulated by, or doing business with, their respective ministries. There are laws and regulations regarding conflict of interest, but they were not enforced. Petty corruption among police, teachers, and other government employees was widespread. Police extorted money from citizens and refugees, and prison officials extorted money from family members of inmates.

<u>Financial Disclosure</u>: The law on public probity requires senior government officials to declare their assets to the attorney general. According to the Ministry of Justice and Human Rights, the financial information of government officials was provided to the appropriate government office. The law treats these reports as confidential. The president, vice president, and president of the National Assembly are exempt from these public probity requirements. Nonexempt government officials are to make a new declaration within 30 days of assuming a new post and every two years thereafter. The law does not stipulate a new declaration be made upon leaving office but states that officials must return all government property within 60 days.

Penalties for noncompliance vary depending on which section of the law was violated but include removal from office, a bar from government employment for three to five years, a ban on contracting with the government for three years, repayment of the illicitly gained assets, and a fine of up to 100 times the value of the accepted bribe. The National Office of Economic Police is responsible for investigating violations of this law, as well as other financial and economic crimes, and then referring them to the Financial Court for prosecution. There were no known cases related to this law during the year.

Transparency problems remained in the diamond industry, particularly regarding allocations of exploration, production, and purchasing rights.

<u>Public Access to Information</u>: The law provides for public access to government information. While the amount of information posted on government websites gradually increased, it remained limited. Laws are made public by being published in the official gazette. The gazette can be purchased for a small fee but was not available online in its entirety. In general the government was not responsive to routine requests for information, and it was sometimes unclear what information the government considered public versus private.

Section 5. Governmental Attitude Regarding International and Nongovernmental Investigation of Alleged Violations of Human Rights

A variety of domestic and international human rights groups operated throughout the country. Some of those investigating government corruption and human rights abuses alleged government interference in their activities. Civil society organizations faced difficulties in contacting detainees, and prison authorities undermined civil society work in the prisons.

The Law of Associations requires NGOs to specify their mandate and areas of activity. The government used this provision to prevent or discourage established NGOs from engaging in certain activities, especially those that the government deemed politically sensitive. In March 2015 a presidential decree meant to regulate NGO operations formalized many of the unenforced requirements of the Law of Associations and restructured the government agency in charge of implementing the law. NGOs cited concern regarding new reporting requirements concerning their activities, financial accounts, and foreign and domestic employees. They also expressed concern about the burden of proving to the government that their activities have a tangible "public benefit." NGOs doing work on political rights and human rights defenders argued the new regulation, and particularly the "public benefit" clause, is specifically meant to limit their work. The Ministry of Justice and Human Rights stated the new regulation was necessary to comply with international financial transparency and anti-money-laundering standards, and that the regulation was not meant to restrict NGO activities.

Even before the new regulation, the government allowed local NGOs to carry out human rights-related work, but many NGOs reported they were forced to limit the scope of their work because they faced problems registering, were subject to subtle forms of intimidation, and risked more serious forms of harassment and closure.

Unlike in previous years, there were no reports that the government arrested and harassed NGO workers.

Government Human Rights Bodies: The state-funded Inter-Ministerial Commission for the Writing of Human Rights Reports includes only representatives from various government ministries. Leading civil society members decided not to participate on the commission because they did not believe it was independent or effective.

The 10th Commission on Human Rights of the National Assembly is charged with investigating citizen complaints of alleged human rights violations and makes recommendations to the National Assembly.

An independent Office of the Ombudsman existed to mediate between an aggrieved public, including prisoners, and an offending public office or institution. The office had no decision-making or adjudicative powers but it helped citizens obtain access to justice and advised government entities on citizen rights. The office also published reports and educated the public about human rights and the role of the ombudsman.

Section 6. Discrimination, Societal Abuses, and Trafficking in Persons

Women

Rape and Domestic Violence: Rape, including spousal rape, is illegal and punishable by up to eight years' imprisonment. Limited investigative resources, poor forensic capabilities, and an ineffective judicial system prevented prosecution of most cases. The government continued a public media campaign highlighting violence against women. The Ministry of Justice and Human Rights worked with the Ministry of Interior to increase the number of female police officers and to improve police response to rape allegations.

On July 26, the newspaper *O Pais* reported, citing statistics from a Luanda hospital, there were 574 reported cases of sexual violence during the first six months of the year at that hospital alone, as compared with 419 cases reported by the Ministries of Family and Protection of Women, Interior, and Social Assistance and Reintegration in 2015. The ministry reported 25,414 incidents of domestic violence in 2015, an increase of 57 percent from 2014.

The Zero Tolerance for Gender and Sexual Based Violence campaign continued. The campaign increased awareness of sexual violence and encouraged women to file police reports.

The law criminalizes domestic violence and penalizes offenders with prison sentences and fines depending on the severity of their crime. In 2015 the government reported it had 27 domestic violence counseling centers, seven other shelters, and various treatment centers throughout the country. It called for more studies into the causes of domestic violence as well as more shelters to help victims. The ministry maintained a program with the Angolan Bar Association to give free legal assistance to abused women and established counseling centers to help families cope with domestic abuse. Statistics on prosecutions for violence against women were not available.

The Organization of Angolan Women (OMA), a political association affiliated with the ruling MPLA, held a series of seminars across the country to increase awareness of the dangers of domestic violence.

<u>Other Harmful Traditional Practices</u>: During the year sporadic news reports of children being accused of witchcraft were published. The National Institute for Religious Affairs acknowledged that belief in, and accusations of, witchcraft continued, particularly in Zaire and Uige provinces, but stated that cases of abusive practices diminished significantly due to campaigns and government directives aimed at reducing indigenous religious practices such as shamanism, animal sacrifices, and witchcraft. There were anecdotal reports of women and children being abused by their communities because of accusations they practiced witchcraft. The Ministry of Culture and the National Institute for Children (INAC) had educational initiatives and emergency programs to assist children accused of witchcraft.

<u>Sexual Harassment</u>: Sexual harassment was common and not illegal. Such cases may be prosecuted under assault and battery and defamation statutes, but no prosecutions were reported during the year.

<u>Reproductive Rights</u>: Couples and individuals have the right to decide freely and responsibly the number, spacing, and timing of their children; manage their reproductive health; and have access to the information and means to do so, free from discrimination, coercion, or violence. According to the UN Population Division, 12 percent of married women used a modern method of contraception. In 2015 the government issued its first-ever national family planning strategy. According to the UN Population Fund's "Trends in Maternal Mortality: 1990--2015", the maternal mortality ratio in 2015 was 477 deaths per 100,000 live births. High maternal mortality was likely due to inadequate access to health facilities before, during, and after giving birth, lack of skilled obstetric care, and early pregnancy.

According to UN sources, 55 percent of women were 18 or younger when they gave birth to their first child. There were no legal barriers that limit access to reproductive health services, but some cultural views, such as the responsibility of women to have children, and religious objections to using contraception, limited access. Comprehensive information on government provisions for reproductive health services or diagnosis and treatment of sexually transmitted infections, including HIV/AIDS, improved with the assistance of international partners.

<u>Discrimination</u>: Under the constitution and law, women enjoy the same rights and legal status as men, but societal discrimination against women remained a problem, particularly in rural areas (see section 7.d.). There were no effective mechanisms

to enforce child support laws, and women generally bore the major responsibility for raising children. There were no known cases of official or private sector discrimination in employment or occupation, credit, pay, owning and/or managing a business, or housing. Gender discrimination was more prevalent in terms of household responsibilities than in access to goods or services.

The law provides for equal pay for equal work (see section 7.d.), although women generally held low-level positions.

In an interministerial effort led by the Ministry of Family and Protection of Women, the government undertook multiple information campaigns on women's rights and domestic abuse and hosted national, provincial, and municipal workshops and training sessions.

Children

Birth Registration: Citizenship is derived by birth within the country or from one's parents. The government does not register all births immediately, and activists reported many urban and rural children remained undocumented. According to the UN Children's Fund, as of mid-2013, as many as 69 percent of children under age five did not have birth certificates. The government permitted undocumented children to attend school but only through the fourth grade. Pursuant to a 2013 plan, the government waived birth registration fees for all persons, including adults, through the end of 2016. In previous years parents could register their children under five for no fee, but parents with older children found the registration costs prohibitive.

Education: Education is tuition-free and compulsory for documented children through the sixth grade, but students often faced significant additional expenses such as books or fees paid to education officials. These fees sometimes were payments to help with school operation and maintenance costs that were not covered by the national budget. At other times, however, the fees were bribes paid by families to ensure their child got a place in a classroom. When parents were unable to pay the fees, their children were often unable to attend school.

Children of any age in an urban area were more likely to attend school than children in a rural area. Children in rural areas generally lacked access to secondary education and often primary level also. Children of refugees and asylum seekers reportedly experienced difficulty enrolling in school due to an inability to procure identification documents. Even in provincial capitals, there were not enough classroom spaces for all children. There were reports that parents, especially in more rural areas, were more likely to send boys to school than girls. According to UNESCO, enrollment rates were higher for boys than for girls, especially at the secondary level.

Child Abuse: Child abuse was widespread. Reports of physical abuse within the family were commonplace, and local officials largely tolerated abuse. Particularly vulnerable children, such as orphans or those without access to health care or education, were more likely to be abused by their caretakers. A 2012 law significantly improved the legal framework protecting children, but problems remained in its implementation and enforcement.

Early and Forced Marriage: The legal age for marriage with parental consent is 15 years. The government did not enforce this restriction effectively, and the traditional age of marriage in lower income groups coincided with the onset of puberty. In September the Ministry of Family and Protection of Women reported that four in 10 children in the country between the ages of 12 and 17 entered annually into legal or common-law marriages, citing rural areas within the provinces of Lunda Sul, Moxico, Huambo, Bie, and Malange as places where early marriage was most prevalent. Data on the rate of marriage for boys and girls under age 18 was not available Common-law marriage was widely practiced.

Sexual Exploitation of Children: All forms of prostitution, including child prostitution, are illegal. Police did not actively enforce laws against prostitution, and local NGOs expressed concern over child prostitution, especially in Luanda, Benguela, and Cunene provinces. Penalties for sexual exploitation of children are defined in a 2014 antitrafficking law that includes protections against child pornography, prostitution, and sexual and labor abuse. The law does not prohibit the use, procurement, offering, and financial benefit of a child for the production of pornography and pornographic performances. The law does not criminally prohibit the distribution and possession of child pornography.

Sexual relations between an adult and a child under the age of 12 are considered rape and carry a potential legal penalty of eight to 12 years' imprisonment. Sexual relations with a child between the ages of 12 and 17 is considered sexual abuse, and convicted offenders may receive sentences from two to eight years in prison. Limited investigative resources and an inadequate judicial system prevented prosecution of most cases. There were no known prosecutions during the year. The legal age for consensual sex is 18 years.

A 2012 law codified the "11 Commitments to Children" campaign. The law defines priorities and coordinates the government's policies to combat all forms of abuse against children, including unlawful child labor, trafficking, and sexual exploitation.

International Child Abductions: The country is not a party to the 1980 Hague Convention on the Civil Aspects of International Child Abduction. See the Department of State's *Annual Report on International Parental Child Abduction* at travel.state.gov/content/childabduction/en/legal/compliance.html.

Anti-Semitism

There is a Jewish community of approximately 350 persons, primarily expatriate Israelis. There were no reports of anti-Semitic acts.

Trafficking in Persons

See the Department of State's *Trafficking in Persons Report* at www.state.gov/j/tip/rls/tiprpt/.

Persons with Disabilities

The law prohibits discrimination against persons with disabilities, including persons with physical, sensory, intellectual, and mental disabilities, in employment (see also section 7.d.), education, and access to health care and the judicial system or other state services, but the government did not effectively enforce these prohibitions. The constitution grants persons with disabilities full rights without restriction and calls on the government to adopt national policies to prevent, treat, rehabilitate, and integrate persons with disabilities to support their families; remove obstacles to their mobility; educate society about disability; and encourage special learning and training opportunities for persons with disabilities. It does not specifically mention the rights of persons with disabilities with regard to transportation, including air travel.

Persons with disabilities included more than 80,000 victims of land mines and other explosive remnants of war. The NGO Handicap International estimated that as many as 500,000 persons had disabilities. Because of limited government resources and uneven availability, only 30 percent of such persons were able to take advantage of state-provided services such as physical rehabilitation, schooling, training, or counseling.

The National Council for Persons with Disabilities is responsible for verifying that all such persons are protected from discrimination and have access to the same rights and privileges as citizens without disabilities. Persons with disabilities, nevertheless, found it difficult to access public or private facilities, and it was difficult for such persons to find employment or participate in the education system (see also section 7.d.). Women with disabilities were reported to be vulnerable to sexual abuse and abandonment when pregnant. The antitrafficking law specifically punishes sexual abuse of vulnerable populations, including persons with disabilities. The Ministry of Assistance and Social Reintegration sought to address problems facing persons with disabilities, including veterans with disabilities, and several government entities supported programs to assist individuals disabled by landmine incidents. During the 2012 election, the government provided voting assistance to persons with disabilities. Persons with disabilities were allowed to select someone of their own choosing to accompany them into the voting booth to fill out the ballot and were allowed to move ahead of others waiting in line to vote.

Indigenous People

An estimated 14,000 San persons lived in small dispersed communities in Huila, Cunene, and Cuando Cubango provinces. The San are traditional hunter-gatherers who are linguistically and ethnically distinct from the majority of the population. The constitution does not make specific reference to the rights of indigenous persons, and the San lacked adequate access to basic government services, including medical care, education, and identification cards, according to a credible NGO. The government reportedly permitted businesses and well-connected elites to take traditional land from the San. During the year NGO sources reported that security guards killed several San individuals who were allegedly hunting on lands that the San had traditionally occupied, but were now occupied by the government or businesses. Many San reportedly turned to begging because other options were not available.

Acts of Violence, Discrimination, and Other Abuses Based on Sexual Orientation and Gender Identity

The constitution prohibits all forms of discrimination but does not specifically address sexual orientation or gender identity. According to the Ministry of Justice and Human Rights, the law does not criminalize sexual relations between persons of the same sex. Sections of the 1886 penal code could be viewed as criminalizing homosexual activity, but they are no longer used by the judicial system. The constitution defines marriage as between a man and a woman, however. Local and international NGOs reported that lesbian, gay, bisexual, transgender, and intersex (LGBTI) individuals faced discrimination and harassment, but reports of violence against the LGBTI community based on sexual orientation were rare. The government, through its health agencies, instituted a series of initiatives to decrease discrimination against LGBTI individuals. For example, the National Institute to Fight HIV/AIDS worked with local NGOs and LGBTI activists to promote antidiscriminatory practices by health practitioners and communities across the country.

Discrimination against LGBTI individuals often went unreported. LGBTI individuals asserted that sometimes police refused to register their grievances. In 2014 a group of LGBTI individuals formed the first openly gay association in civil society. The association was created to help LGBTI youth facing harassment or social alienation. During the year the association partnered with the Ministry of Health and the National Institute to Fight HIV/AIDS to improve access to health services and sexual education for the LGBTI community.

HIV and AIDS Social Stigma

Discrimination against those with HIV/AIDS is illegal, but lack of enforcement allowed employers to discriminate against persons with the condition or disease. There were no news reports of violence against persons with HIV/AIDS. Reports from local and international health NGOs suggested discrimination against individuals with HIV/AIDS was common. The government's National Institute to Fight HIV/AIDS includes sensitivity and antidiscrimination training for its employees when they are testing and counseling HIV patients. Local NGOs worked with the government to combat stigmatization and discrimination against persons with HIV/AIDS.

Section 7. Worker Rights

a. Freedom of Association and the Right to Collective Bargaining

The law provides for the right of workers, except members of the armed forces and police, to form and join independent unions. To establish a trade union, at least 30 percent of workers in an economic sector in a province must follow a registration process and obtain authorization from government officials. The law provides for the right to collective bargaining except in the civil service. The law prohibits strikes by members of the armed forces, police, prosecutors and magistrates of the

PGR, prison staff, fire fighters, public sector employees providing "essential services," and oil workers.

While the law allows unions to conduct their activities without government interference, it also places some restrictions on their ability to strike. Before engaging in a strike, workers must make a good-faith effort to negotiate their grievances with their employer. Should they fail to negotiate the government can deny the right to strike. The government may intervene in labor disputes that affect national security and energy sectors. Essential services are broadly defined, including the transport sector, communications, waste management and treatment, and fuel distribution. In exceptional circumstances involving national interests, authorities have the power to requisition workers in the essential services sector. Collective labor disputes are to be settled through compulsory arbitration by the Ministry of Public Administration, Employment, and Social Security. The law does not prohibit employer retribution against strikers, and it permits the government to force workers back to work for "breaches of worker discipline" or participation in unauthorized strikes. Nonetheless, the law prohibits antiunion discrimination and stipulates that worker complaints should be adjudicated in the labor court. By law employers are required to reinstate workers who have been dismissed for union activities. There were no known cases of retribution against strikers during the year.

The government generally did not effectively enforce applicable laws. The Ministry of Public Administration, Employment, and Social Security had a hotline for workers who believed their rights had been violated, and the leader of the Confederation of Free and Independent Labor Unions of Angola, an independent labor confederation, stated in 2014 that the labor courts functioned, albeit slowly. Enforcement efforts were hampered by an insufficient number of adequately trained labor inspectors. In 2015 there were 187 labor inspectors for the country. Some companies were reportedly tipped off on impending labor inspections, making government efforts ineffective.

Freedom of association and the right to collective bargaining were not generally respected. Government approval is required to form and join unions, which were hampered by membership and legalization issues. Labor unions, independent of those run by the government, worked to increase their influence, but the ruling MPLA continued to dominate the labor movement due to historical connections between the party and labor, and also the superior financial base of the country's largest labor union (which also constitutes the labor wing of the MPLA). The government is the country's largest employer, and the Ministry of Public

Administration, Employment, and Social Security mandated government worker wages with no negotiation with the unions.

Various worker strikes occurred in different parts of the country during the year. For example, according to press reports, on August 25, more than 2,000 employees went on strike at the port of Lobito, the country's second largest port, to demand payment of four months of salary arrears. Port authorities and the workers union reportedly resolved the strike after one week on the condition of immediate payment of one month of salary arrears followed by the remaining salary arrears two months later. On September 22, workers at the port initiated a second strike after the authorities failed to deliver on the payment of the salary arrears. Workers reportedly suspended the strike on September 28 after a new plan to pay their salary arrears was implemented.

b. Prohibition of Forced or Compulsory Labor

The law prohibits all forms of forced or compulsory labor.

The government did not effectively enforce the law due in part to an insufficient number of inspectors. Penalties for violations are the same as those for trafficking in persons, ranging from eight to 12 years in prison, and may be insufficient to deter violations.

Forced labor occurred among men and women in agriculture, construction, domestic service, and artisanal diamond-mining sectors, particularly in Lunda Norte and Lunda Sul provinces. Migrant workers were subject to seizure of passports, threats, denial of food, and confinement. The government continued to make use of a training video for law enforcement and immigration officials that included a short segment on how to identify victims of trafficking, although this was not the sole objective of the film. INAC continued working to reduce the number of children traveling to agricultural areas in the country's southern regions to work on farms, mostly through community outreach about the importance of an education. Forced child labor also occurred.

See also the Department of State's *Trafficking in Persons Report* at www.state.gov/j/tip/rls/tiprpt/.

c. Prohibition of Child Labor and Minimum Age for Employment

The law prohibits children under 14 from working. To obtain an employment contract, the law requires youth to submit evidence they are 14 years of age or older. Children could work from age 14 to 16 with parental permission or without parental consent if they are married and the work did not interfere with schooling or harm the physical, mental, and moral development of the minor. The law also allows orphan children that want to work to get official permission in the form of a letter from "an appropriate institution" but does not specify the type of institution. The Ministries of Public Administration, Employment, and Social Security; Social Assistance and Reintegration; and Interior; INAC; and the national police are the entities responsible for enforcement of child labor laws. A new interministerial commission to combat trafficking in persons was created in 2014 to coordinate enforcement actions. The commission generally effectively enforced child labor standards in the formal sector, but the government had difficulty monitoring the large informal sector, where most children worked.

Inspectors are authorized to conduct surprise inspections whenever they see fit. Penalties for violations were generally sufficient to deter violations. Penalties for not signing a written contract for children ages 14 and over is a fine of two to five times the median monthly salary offered by the company. Children over age 14 who are employed as part of an apprenticeship are also required to have a written contract. The penalty for not having this contract is three to six times the average monthly salary of the company. For children found to be working in jobs categorized as hazardous (which is illegal under the law), the fines are five to 10 times the average monthly salary of the company. Nonpayment of any of these fines results in the accrual of additional fines.

Child labor, especially in the informal sector, remained a problem. The Ministry of Public Administration, Employment, and Social Security had oversight of formal work sites in all 18 provinces, but it was unknown if inspectors checked on the age of workers or conditions of work sites. If the ministry determined a business was using child labor, it transferred the case to the Ministry of Interior to investigate and possibly press charges. It was not known if the government fined any businesses for using child labor. The Ministry of Public Administration, Employment, and Social Security, other government agencies, and labor unions developed a national plan to limit child labor. In June the deputy attorney general reported that authorities interdicted one bus with 20 children on board in Bie Province as the bus traveled toward Luanda Province, reportedly to supply child laborers to a farm. Authorities arrested the driver, and the case was under investigation at year's end.

Generally, work done by children was in the informal sector. Children engaged in economic activities such as agricultural labor on family farms and commercial plantations--particularly in orchards--as well as in fishing, brick making, charcoal production, domestic labor, and street vending. Exploitive labor practices included involvement in the sale, transport, and offloading of goods in ports and across border posts. Children were reportedly forced to act as couriers in the illegal cross-border trade with Namibia. Adult criminals sometimes used children for forced criminal activity, since the justice system prohibits youths under 12 from being tried in court. There were no credible reports of the use of child labor and forced child labor in informal diamond mining.

Street work among children was common, especially in the provinces of Luanda, Benguela, Huambo, Huila, and Kwanza Sul. Investigators found children working in the streets of Luanda, but many returned during the weekends to some form of dwelling in Luanda or outlying cities. Most of these children shined shoes, washed cars, carried water and other goods, or engaged in other informal labor, but some resorted to petty crime and begging. Commercial sexual exploitation of children occurred as well.

The government, through INAC, worked to create, train, and strengthen child protection networks at the provincial and municipal levels in all 18 provinces. No central mechanism existed to track cases or provide statistics. In 2015, in Benguela, Lunda Sul, and Bengo provinces, local authorities uncovered 68 cases of child labor, but there were no reported prosecutions. The government also dedicated resources to the expansion of educational and livelihood opportunities for children and their families.

Also see the Department of Labor's *Findings on the Worst Forms of Child Labor* at www.dol.gov/ilab/reports/child-labor/findings/.

d. Discrimination with Respect to Employment and Occupation

The labor law prohibits discrimination in employment and occupation based on race, sex, religion, disability, or language, and the government in general effectively enforced the law in the formal sector. The constitution prohibits all forms of discrimination, although it does not specifically address political opinion, national origin, sexual orientation, or gender identity (see section 6). The law provides for equal pay for equal work, and many women held high-level positions in state-run industries and in the private sector or worked in the informal sector. There were no known prosecutions of official or private sector gender-based discrimination in employment or occupation. Women have held and continued to hold ministerial posts.

Despite the law, persons with disabilities found it difficult to gain access to public or private facilities, and it was difficult for such persons to participate in the education system and thus find employment. There were no known reports of discrimination in employment or occupation.

Discrimination against migrant workers also occurred.

e. Acceptable Conditions of Work

The minimum wage in the trade and extractive industries sectors is 22,495 kwanza ($132) per month, 18,750 kwanza ($110) in the transportation, services and manufacturing sectors, and 15,003 kwanza ($88) in the agriculture sector. The minimum wage law does not cover workers in informal sectors, such as street vendors, subsistence farmers, and domestic servants. The country had not established a poverty income level; however, the UN Development Program estimated the poverty level to be 165 kwanzas ($1) per day, or 4,950 kwanzas ($29) per month.

The standard workweek is 44 hours with at least one unbroken period of 24 hours of rest per week. When employees engage in shift work or a variable weekly schedule, they may work up to 54 hours per week before the employer must pay overtime. In the formal sector, there is a prohibition on excessive compulsory overtime, defined as more than two hours a day, 40 hours a month, or 200 hours a year. The law also provides for paid annual holidays. By law employers must provide, at a minimum, a 50 percent of monthly salary bonus to employees in December and an annual vacation. Workweek standards were not enforced unless employees lodged a formal complaint with the Ministry of Public Administration, Employment, and Social Security (MAPTSS). Foreign workers with permanent legal status or a temporary work visa were protected under the labor law.

MAPTSS effectively enforced the minimum wage law within the formal labor sector. An estimated 60 percent of the economy derives from the informal sector and most wage earners held second jobs or depended on the agricultural or other informal sectors to augment their incomes. Most workers in the informal sector were not covered by wage or occupational safety standards.

On August 9, Presidential Decree 15/16 entered into force establishing minimum employment standards for domestic workers, including national minimum wage protection; an eight-hour work day for domestic workers living outside of their employer's home; a 10-hour work day for domestic workers living inside their employer's home; compulsory employer contributions to a domestic worker's social security protection; and maternity and holiday allowances. MAPTSS is charged with implementing and enforcing the law.

The labor law guarantees a safe work environment in all sectors of the economy. Employees have the right to remove themselves from hazardous working conditions and may file a formal complaint with MAPTSS if employers insist they perform hazardous tasks. The government enforced occupational safety and health standards and investigated private company operations based on complaints made by NGOs.